Glimpses of a Fractured Soul

Mercedes Lewis

Troubadour Books
by Regal Crest

Tennessee

Copyright © 2017 by Mercedes Lewis

All rights reserved. No part of this publication may be reproduced, transmitted in any form or by any means, electronic or mechanical, including photocopy, recording, or any information storage and retrieval system, without permission in writing from the publisher. The characters, incidents and dialogue herein are fictional and any resemblance to actual events or persons, living or dead, is purely coincidental.

ISBN 978-1-61929-326-7

First Printing 2017

9 8 7 6 5 4 3 2 1

Original cover design by AcornGraphics
Cover image by Cole Armocida

Published by:

Regal Crest Enterprises
1042 Mount Lebanon Rd
Maryville, TN 37804

Find us on the World Wide Web at
http://www.regalcrest.biz

Published in the United States of America

Advance Praise for *Glimpses of a Fractured Soul*:

These are the songs of Mercedes Lewis, true to herself and her life. They are unique in style, and in form. As she writes in her poem "Keep Up," "I love to rhyme/ though some poets/ look at me as if/ it is a crime."

Defiant, too, about meter, I call meter visceral rhythm and we've all got our own. Mercedes Lewis will not have anyone imposing their rhythm on her. "Reading," is one of my favorites: "Are you reading/ what I think I wrote,/ or/ are you reading/ what you need to believe/ My world, colored/ by your crayons." The poems are Lewis' unique voice — very personal, inspirational, courageous, sometimes deep, sometimes funny — her voice is strong and Im grateful to hear it.

~ **Lee Lynch, Author**

From the tearjerker of a "dedication" holding a plethora of names and a collection of emotions, to the comedic porcelain Queen, I began my journey through the poems of a friend. Onward I travel. Through the erotic innuendo-decorated alleyways inhabited by a woman who can slay without killing, holding the gift of a little death in her hands. As I meander, I glance in the windows built by words. I inhale scents, savour tastes and catch the occasional glimpse of a soul once fractured that lives in the memory of this extraordinary poet. I even recognised someone I met once.

Mercedes Lewis runs the gamut of emotion in this, her debut book. The poet hopes to take us, the readers on a journey. She does ... but it is one urged, compelled and inspired by her own journeys. This is what makes a poet worthy of being read. I'm so glad I took the time to take a trip with Mercedes.

~ **Chris Parsons, Author**

Glimpses of a Fractured Soul is a polished, yet raw collection of poems that linger. In "Touching Live Wire" and "Blues and Soul," Mercedes Lewis finds the beauty and strength in confronting pain. In "Keep Up," she engages and challenges the reader to look beyond the rhymes to the soul-wrenching imagery. This celebration of language and living transforms suffering into joy and the prosaic into the imaginative.

~ **Elizabeth Andersen, host of the Sandra Moran Radio Book Club**

Acknowledgements

It takes a lifetime to live a life. I am not finished yet, but thank you to all the people who have influenced my life thus far along the way.

My publisher and my editor have infinite patience. Cathy had years of persistence and patience in encouraging me. I finished much of the writing ages ago; it was the fear that held me back. For me, writing poetry is a solitary, cathartic and personal endeavor, and the level of emotional exposure almost paralyzed me. Nevertheless, I have decided; those that see me see me anyway.

Thank you, Cindy, for your encouragement, and your editorial eye.

I hope every reader who picks up this book, even if only for a moment, glimpses themselves somewhere within.

Dedication

To Floretta, "little flower" who bloomed fully and lived a large life in a small space of time. Thank you, Mama. I miss you so much.

To Joseph, "he will add", gracious enough to be pained when he learned that all he meant for good did not turn out so. Nonetheless, in the end, ALL IS WELL. Thank you, Daddy.

To Stella, "my star", you were my angel, my savior, my advocate. Thank you for saving my life, for saving me.

To the Culps, for prayer, for not giving up on me, and for delivering me to the "work it out" hospital. How old am I again? LOL

To Andrea, "beautiful lady, little warrior", my saving grace. Thank you for choosing me as your mama, thereby helping to bring calm from chaos, beauty from ashes, and restoration and redemption to a bruised and fractured soul.

I love you all.

Table of Contents

Chapter One - Life Is Fun and Funny

Style	2
Microwave	3
Partners	4
My Queen	5
For All of Us	6
Circular	7
Season's Greetings	8
Cooking 101	9
Beauty	10
Blue	11
Silver Bullet	12
Shopping	13
SLEEP	14
Homage to My Hairstylist	15
Con Fun	16
Autocorrect (I type, it types)	17

Chapter Two - Women and Such

Bits and Pieces	19
Mindset	20
Kaleidoscope	21
Horse and Pony Show	22
Certainty	23
Finally	24

Her	25
Not Mine to Give	26
Last Dance	27
Is Chivalry Dead?	28
She Clung to Me	29
Let's Keep it Straight	30
Peach Tree	31
The Professor	32
Thoughts	33
A Soft Hard Woman	34
Lavender Descends	35
You Slay Me	36
Fog	37
Tell Me Lies	38
Understanding	39
What a Ride	40

Chapter Three - Family Matters

For Grandmother	42
The Last to Know	43
Her Story	44
February 17th	46
The Promise	47
The Scapegoat	48

Too Much Stuff	49
ISSUES	50
Little Sisters	52
Time Stands Still	53
Seven	54
Good Times	55
I will always protect you	56
Star	57
Oatmeal	58
Trey	59
Oh Daddy	60
The Savior	61
DCBR	62
Mother and Daughter	64
Varied Responses	65

Chapter Four - Glimpses

Glimpses of a Fractured Soul:	
Touching Live Wire	68
Triboluminescence	70
Because	71
Adrift	72
Again	73
Bad Hair Sunday	74

Blues and Soul	75
But, Realize	76
Darkness Came First	77
Few words	78
Fallen Leaves, Lost Sisters	80
God's Child	81
Handwriting on the Wall	82
Help	83
I Do Me	84
I see you, Sister	86
In Retrospect	87
Infinity	88
Praise	89
Keep Up	90
Lois' Poetry	91
Reading	92
Monday Morning	93
My Haiku	94
The telling	95
My New Rainbow	96
My Thing	97
Night	98
That Day	99

Relationships	100
Nothing	101
On Being a Poet	102
Peaceful	104
Just Don't	105
Uniquely Mine	106
Playa	107
Thy Name	108
Should BE	109
Sowing	110
Tend Your Own Garden	111
Three Things (Because there are always three things	112
Victor	113

Chapter One

Life is Fun and Funny

Style

Row upon row,
aisle upon aisle,
looking for that perfect fit,
looking for my style.

A little bit of this,
a little bit of that,
odds and ends to make a whole,
throw on a fancy hat.

Jewels that sparkle,
boots that gleam, put on a tiara,
and step out like a queen.

A tie, a fedora
some slats, or stacks,
some thought femme yesterday,
today, taken aback.

Now THAT is style!

Microwave

It's a simple thing really
and it shouldn't drive me crazy
and I'm sure she doesn't do it
because she's mean or cuz she's lazy

After all of this time
and the things that we've been through
you would think that by now
she would know just what to do

Please
RESET the fucking microwave

Partners

In sickness and in health,
is what the words say.
So, even in illness,
we'll stay together anyway.

When we are older,
and our backs won't bend,
our knees won't raise,
or our hips won't mend.
When our arms are too short,
and our legs are too long,
we'll need someone's help
To get our socks on.

I'm glad you will be there.

My Queen

When I stumble in after a
night of debauchery,
she is there, waiting
for me.
No judgment.
I subjugate myself,
to her,
resting my head on her.
She is cool to the touch.
So refreshing,
so welcoming.
I hug her closely,
and give her my
deepest offering.
She willingly accepts.
My porcelain queen.

For All of Us

As we grow older,
one thing we *must* have,
is someone with whom to grow older
and laugh.

Laugh at each other,
laugh at ourself,
but no matter what,
don't climb up on a shelf.

When drivers think your car
is the kind that you bump,
and one of you is sporting
a shiner or lump,
when your body aches,
and your teeth fall out,
it's really good to have
someone about,
to remind you of when
you could catch a ball,
or sport 5-inch heels
without taking a fall.

It may be a brother,
or lover, or friend,
but with this one person
there'll be no pretend.

No matter what else you forget,
make a deal,
to laugh right out loud
now and then,
til you squeal.

Circular

Sit here, grasshopper,
I'll teach you a thing or two,
add some wisdom to your living,
to live better than I do.

I will teach you many lessons,
some you'll grasp, some you won't.
You will get your bumps and bruises
learning those things that you don't.

Sit here, grasshopper, now,
and let me learn from you.
Yes, the teacher is the student,
and the student teaches, too.

Season's Greetings

Happy winter, spring, summer or fall.
I feel that there are reasons we should celebrate them all.

Each has its own charm, each one, its own reason.
There is cause to celebrate, and find joy in each new season.

Winter brings us holidays, for giving thanks, and to receive.
Goodwill, gifts and family are all reasons to believe.

Starry night and warm showers, hoping new life to bring,
are but two special happenings which alert us that it's spring.

Heat, beaches, pests and sand all herald in sweet summer.
If no water is nearby, it could really be a bummer.

Cooling breezes of autumn, as the leaves begin to fall,
reminds us of the sweetness, and the beauty of it sll.

So, welcome in each season, with its happy, and its sad.
Just remember there's no season that can truly be all bad.

Celebrate each new season, its course in life to chart.
Make special memories every day, and keep them in your heart.

Cooking 101

Everything you cook
doesn't have to be on high.
Everything you cook
doesn't need to boil or fry.

Back that heat up,
slow it down.
Some things should be
a little brown.
Some things simmer, braise, or steam,
some things should still be brightly green.

Pan sear, sauté, muddle, reduce
all are ways to cook.
You can cook by trial and error,
or, you can use a book.

If you cannot relax,
and enjoy the cooking craze,
save the pots and pans,
and just use the microwave.

Beauty

Beauty is a strange thing,
to which it doesn't matter,
what ugly place it finds itself,
what chaos, or what clatter.

Beauty is found in peace,
beauty is found in war,
it's deep beneath the sea and,
on eagle's wings it'll soar.

Beauty is found in girls,
and yes, beauty is found in boys.
Beauty's found in quiet, still,
and beauty's found in noise.

Beauty is found in others,
who have yet to decide,
how much of self is beauty,
and how much self to hide.

Beauty is in the mind,
and, beauty's in the body.
Beauty is in the things we do,
some nice, and some, seem naughty.

Beauty is a strange thing
no one can find for you.
Beauty is what you make it,
so, unto thine self, be true.

Blue

I want to write a happy song,
I really, really do.
But, each time I put pen to paper,
words just come out...blue.

It's not the type of happy song
you might be used to hearing.
Minor chords of pain
make this song oh so endearing.

Born of a fresh new love,
dropped from the nest too soon,
no other song to build upon,
I made my own strange tune.

See, I know why the caged bird sang,
and though she was set free,
those things still buried deep within
will never cease to be.

So, hear in this,
my happy song.
It's different,
but it is not wrong.

And, if your happy song seems sad,
or just a little blue,
forget what others say, or think,
and sing your blue song, too.

Silver Bullet

No, my dear,
not the one you're thinking of
though I love that silver bullet
most especially with my love.

No, not that one either
although you could win a bet
after that silver bullet
I might need a cigarette.

Not that silver bullet either,
but I hear it is a blast
when you're really in a hurry
and you need to get there fast.

Yes, that one, darling
and it's true what they say
that to end a werewolf fantasy
it is the only way.
Ouch.

Shopping

Got what I needed,
did the self checkout line,
now I'm sitting here waiting
as you lag along behind.

In and out, in and out,
is the way we said we'd be,
not a stroll up and down each aisle
to see what we could see!

Don't try to persuade me,
don't try to change my mood,
I'm done with this, I tell you,
now I really want some food.

You can just go ahead,
let me sit here and rest.
For the sake of peace and harmony,
that truly would be best.

SLEEP

Sweet

Languishing

Elusive

Energizing

Powerful

Sleep. I wish I could.

Homage to My Hairstylist

While combing my hair
I found a split end,
which made me wonder,
when I would see you again.

My roots are screaming
bloody murder, they cry
Because I'm in need
of a fresh hair dye.

Now those holidays are over,
and the fun is all done,
I find myself wondering
if I will be the one.

Dye, wash, condition, massage,
has me singing this little homage.
Hair stylist, hair stylist, my talented dear,
please make me lovely, I say with a tear.

Con Fun

Another Con,
another year,
with happy Brits,
and room-temp beer.

More Coffee Chats,
and authors to pursue,
I get all of this,
and lesbians too.

Old and new friends,
skits and a dance.
One might even find
that elusive romance.

Awards,
readings,
membership pins,
keynote speakers who bring us grins.

I'm so glad I found this salvation.

Autocorrect (I type, it types)

Worrier
Warrior

Dies
Does

Love
Live

Worrier dies, love.
Warrior, does live.

Chapter Two

Women and Such

Bits and Pieces

If what they say is true,
then I am bits and pieces...

bits of my first love,
pieces of another,
I guess, in reflection,
I am the sum of all my lovers.

Does it have to hurt
so much,
when they leave,
and I am
in bits
and
pieces?

Mindset

Forgive me
forgive me she said
eyes glistening with
unshed tears chin quivering

How could I have known
it was not the first time
How could I accept
that it would not be the last

Marry me she said
but, I said, as far
as I am concerned
we were already married

Years ago she showed up
on my doorstep her marriage over
she left her husband for you
a dear friend said

No, she did not
I would never allow that
I would never cause that
I would never accept that

But in her mind...

And so like grandmother said
the way you get them
is the same way you lose them

Kaleidoscope

The warm yellow glow of friendship,
shy smiles, talking, laughter, laughter,
and more laughter.

The pink blush of budding romance,
subtle glances, gentle touches, shy smiles,
and the first kiss.

Love bursts forth, vibrating orange,
verdant green, a growing, living thing, this love.

Quenching blue, as I drink of you,
red, hot passionate nights.

Red, puffy eyes, orange flames leaping,
burning off the chaff.

A confusion of colors, going round and round,
sometimes fading to black.

And then,
The warm yellow glow, of new friendship…

Horse and Pony Show

You'll love riding the horse
she said, as she harnessed
up the pony.

She was right.
We rode hard,
well into the night,
and sometimes even into morning.
She would not let me ride
the pony, no matter how I pleaded.
And then she left,
taking her horse and pony with her.

I got my own horse and pony,
and a new rider.
Now, I ride whichever, I choose.

Certainty

Well,
this is not the first
mistake I've ever made.
And, I can say,
with absolute certainty,
it will not be the last.
I only ask that you
walk with me,
talk with me,
bear with me,
care with me,
as I continue this journey of life,
learning as I go.

Finally

Finally.
I cried for you.
It was the deep, sorrowful,
soul-wrenching sound
only the heartbroken can make.
Now, I can move on.
Finally.

Her

She sent me flowers,
beautiful flowers,
with just a blush of color.
They look like her.

She sent me flowers,
with just a hint of scent,
that climbed my nose,
and permeated my senses.
They smell like her.

She sent me flowers,
they are tall and beautiful,
strong and tough, yet soft to the touch.
They feel like her.

She sent me flowers
that are unbreakable and hardy,
born out of adversity.
They *are* like her.

She sent me flowers
that reach across the room,
assault my heart, and soften it.

I did not taste them.
I wonder,
if they taste like her.

I would rather have her.

Not Mine to Give

The situation is pretty grim,
makes me think I should retire,
since she broke my heart in pieces,
and she stole all of my fire.

I wish I had something,
just a little piece to give,
a small piece you could nurture,
'til it gained the will to live.

I wish I could say,
take it, take another
little piece of my heart,

But alas, woe is me, it is not mine to give.

Last Dance

Last dance,
what last dance?
I never even had a chance,
to know it was the last dance.

I would have held you closer,
and savored every word,
had I known they were the last words
from your lips I would have heard.

You could have used your thumb,
to wipe away my tears.
We could have reminisced of all the
good times through the years.

Like, remember the first time you used your thumb?
Bliss

I would have cherished those last moments,
that's all I would have asked.
But you didn't truly know me,
thought me not up to the task.

I know what love is darling.
I know the ebb and flow.
I know you can't hold on to it,
when love chooses to go.

I am a phoenix, my love.
ALWAYS rising up from the ashes.

Is Chivalry Dead?

I must live in a fantasy.
Is chivalry dead?
Please someone tell me.

She didn't open the door.
She didn't hold my chair.
She didn't help me up
or down the stair.

No flowers, no chocolate,
Not one single daisy.
Am I tripping?
Am I crazy?

What's wrong with this butch?
I mean, well damn.
Doesn't she know the caliber
of femme that I am?

As we walked,
she stayed on the inside,
I said nothing, in order
to save her pride.

Is it just me?
Is it all in my head?
Are the days of chivalry long gone?
Dead?

She Clung to Me

Headed out for a stroll
along the familiar streets of PTown
I walk the cobbled streets
perusing the familiar shops
I spy a friend across the way
and cross over for a hug

She clung to me
a wonderful full body hug
I tried to release
She clung to me still
encasing cocooning
and healing me
She took me in
I held until she released

I'm okay
Is she okay
I don't know
I should have asked

Let's Keep it Straight

Now it's time for you to go,
and I haven't said goodbye.
So I hide in the corner,
trying so hard not to cry.

Life is funny,
You are my best friend.
How could I love a woman
who is only into men!

My heart is foolish,
these thoughts I have aren't cool.
These tears will keep on flowing,
but I will not break my rule.

Look at you,
looking at me,
like a trapped animal
that wants to be set free.

I refuse to lose you, friend,
to the thing you think is sin.
There would so much to treasure,
but just one way it could end.

I won't go there,
won't be used as a whim.
so if you want me darling,
then you must be free of him.

Peach Tree

I love the peach fruit,
but I want the whole damn tree.
The tree is life, strength, cover,
and protection for me.

The tree guarantees fruit
for more than just a season.
The fruit calls you out,
But it's only for one reason.

Eat me, it demands.
The fruit is sweet, succulent,
as it drips upon my tongue,
but in just a little while,
all its essence will be gone.

The tree puts down roots,
to hold fast, and it blooms,
dancing with color,
offering fruit for many moons.

I want the peach tree.

The Professor

Snug, lightly faded, neatly frayed jeans,
that surely must have their own doctorate.
Checkered, long sleeve, button down shirt,
red bow tie,
and a fedora.
Please, oh please.
Teach me.

Thoughts

I thought she was plastic when first we met.
Not the soft, pliable plastic, but the hard, brittle,
unyielding plastic, the kind that breaks if you bend it.
What is she hiding? What is she running from?

Better than being paper, I thought,
easily soiled, easily bruised,
easily molded, easily ruined,
unable to withstand anything.

But, my mistake.
I've found that she is wood.
Strong wood, with rings of age, and experience,
warmed by the sun, shapeable, but, almost unbreakable.

Able to stand through
the storm alone, but willing
to hold, protect, and support others.

There are scars, cut, etched into her soul.
They add to her beauty, they do not weaken her.
She does not flinch when you touch them.

But, one does not get in easily.
Like the warmth of the sun, like water,
she will soak you up slowly, absorb you,
absorb you, allow you to penetrate deeply.

I thought she was plastic, or paper.
I was so wrong.
All of her running and hiding is done.
She is petrified wood, softening around the edges.

I should apologize to her.
But, she doesn't know my thoughts.

A Soft Hard Woman

She is a soft, hard woman.
One with strength, and muscles,
but does not get into tussles.

She has the kindest heart you've ever known,
but is able to stand up on her own.

She is firm, yet gentle.
When you touch her just right, she melts.

She is a soft, hard woman.

Lavender Descends

Breathing deeply
lavender descends
floating down, a butterfly
strong as the wind
restless as the tide
light as a feather
delicate as a flower
sharp as a thorn.
Lavender descends,
drifting down
clouding my mind
My eyes are misty
thinking
of you

You Slay Me

Cascading
    falling
        spiraling
            floating
                tripping
                      dripping
                          down

I am tongue-tied
You slay me
Your eyes
Your mouth
Your beautiful curls
Your scent
Your soul
Your hands
Oh god,
those beautiful strong hands
I am spent
You slay me

Fog

Like a heavy fog
memories of her
roll over me
trapping me
in a sweet
savor
that
will not
be
forgotten
Paralyzed
I cannot move forward
to a now
that bears
no comparison
And yet
a light misting fog
and still
I hope
for new reign

Tell me Lies

Tell me lies.
Fiction is hope.
I want hope.
I need hope.
So,
tell me lies.

Understanding

I vacillate,
between pain, anger,
and understanding.
I hope understanding
reigns supreme.

What a Ride

From chat room
to instant message,
to private chat,
have you ever met a woman like that?

Daytona Beach,
toes in the sand.
sex on the first date,
man oh man!

Coast to coast,
foreign places too,
life was so exciting
as my love for her grew.

Space, time, distance,
could not compete,
her hugs and kisses
were oh so sweet.

Wait, she wants to end it now?
But we had just begun.
Was I the only one
who was really having fun?

Like every ride
at the fair,
you just got on,
and then, you're there.

But what a ride!

Chapter Three

Family Matters

For Grandmother

I send you cards and flowers,
while you can see and smell.
I tell you that I love you,
while you can hear, as well.

I touch your face, caress your brow,
while you can smile and feel,
absorb your wisdom, cherish your words,
each moment is so real.

Our treasure is this life
is the souls we come to know.
We are sad and broken-hearted
when our precious ones must go.

We must not lose faith
when the Great One calls one home,
it is a fate we each must keep,
and each will keep alone.

So, there's no need to fuss,
when it is time to leave, we must.
It is His timing, and His will,
and so we should just trust.

I love you Gramma, this know,
not cuz the bible tells me so.
I love because you were and ARE,
and though you leave, you won't be far.

You are always in my heart,
as you have been, from the start.

So as we pass this way in life,
it seems through turmoil, joy and strife;
we smell, touch, feel, and show,
love is life's blessing for all to know.

The Last to Know

It's okay darling, said grandma,
patting me on my knee.
It's okay baby,
There's one in every family.

I thought she meant my cousin.
Fey, fey, so gay Lee,
The gayest baby
you ever did see.

My world fell apart,
my girl and I were through,
I wasn't quite sure
What I was gonna do.

Grandma looked at me boldly,
stared me straight in the eye.
You know, that kind of look she gives
when daring you to lie?

That's okay love,
there's one in every family.
All those years ago,
She was talking about me.

I didn't know she knew.

Smiling I realized that I was the last to know,
that everyone knew.

Her Story

Too black to be white
too white to be black
no zipper to get out
of this skin she's in
Nope, neither side has been easy
Where does she stand?

She can tell you about the black child
feeling motherless
She can tell you about the black girl
feeling lost
She can tell you about the black woman
finding a way to make it work
She can tell you about the black female soldier
hiding in plain sight
She can tell you about the black mother
full of wonder pride and fear
Oh God, the fear

She can tell you, looking into a
mirror darkly, that there is peril
on both sides

On one side
she has a drug addiction problem
They said, I never expected this from you.
She said, do you really think it was a part
of my five year plan
One the other side, she is a crackhead
They never expected it either

Too black to be white
too white to be black
no zipper to get out
of this skin she's in
Nope, neither side has been easy
Where does she stand?

On either side
she is timid yet strong
On either side,
there is love and loss,
laughter and tears,
fear and hope

Too black to be white
too white to be black
no zipper to get out
of this skin she's in
Nope, neither side has been easy
Where does she stand?

Why must she choose a side
Why must anyone
Why must we wrestle
with ourselves and others

Too black to be white
too white to be black
no zipper to get out
of this skin she's in
Nope, neither side has been easy
Where does she stand?

when
can
we
just
BE

February 17th

Such a momentous occasion
yet no different than yesterday
or the day before
no different yet
as different as
the sun and the moon
as different as
night and day
as different as
wet and dry
as different as
hard and soft
how can it be so different
in all its sameness
blessed with fifteen more years
than Mama and yet
it feels no different

The Promise

He peered across the table at me
after a masterfully executed
hand of pinochle
We were knocking them down

Promise me, he said, promise me
Promise you what, I asked puzzled
wondering if I had made a mistake
in our hand

Promise me you will never use heroin
Don't even touch it
Don't even smell it
Promise me
You think too much like me
You think too much, like me
Promise me

He died many years ago
I have kept that promise

The Scapegoat

The straw that broke
the camel's back.
The one too many.
The reason her love would never return,
or so she chose to believe.
The reason her life was ruined.
The reason she could not
stand to look at him.
The reason he bore the brunt
of all her anger, hate and fear.
The reason he rarely felt her love.
The reason, no matter what,
no matter how hard we try,
he will never feel secure
that he is enough,
prayed for,
cared for,
loved,
or worthy.
He is.

Too Much Stuff

She had been visiting two weeks,
and signs pointed to time being up.
You've got too much stuff, he said,
struggling to get past suitcases and gain access to a closet.

Her heart was immediately pierced.
He did not realize how he had just wounded her,
how he opened up a very old hurt,
painfully pulling the scab off of very old sores.

She began to get small right away,
placing all her belongings in the suitcases,
lining them up symmetrically, by size, large to small,
near the bed, not touching any walls,
prayerfully not in any path.

She had felt this way all her life.
As if she had nowhere to belong,
as though she were always an outsider,
as though she were not a part OF.

She closed herself in the room,
sitting on the bed quietly,
making as little noise as possible,
barely daring to breathe.

She had two weeks remaining.
She hoped they would pass peacefully.
She would make no demands.
He would hardly know she was still there.

ISSUES

Issues,
yes, I have them.
I told my brother to "Kiss my BLACK ass."
Is there EVER a reason to say such a thing to your
brother?
Perhaps not, but let me explain.

He used four little trigger words in one message.
ALWAYS, NEVER, US and YOU.
With those four little words, he reached in
and awakened the sleeping two year old deep within,
the two year old who may never fully heal.

Most often, she lies dormant,
in the fetal position,
sucking her thumb,
watching the world go by.

He reached in and snatched the scab off a very old
wound.
He stirred memories of separation, and police, and
aloneness, and searching.
He drove a wedge in a chasm that has been under repair
a lifetime.
He made her realize the world of difference between
them.
STILL.

So, yes, I said it for her.
I apologized. I even tried to explain for her.
He said, you are too old to be hanging on to that shit.
Get over it. Move on.

He tells me these things, but has he?
I am sure he will keep that message a long time.
However, not for as long, I am also certain,
as that little girl inside.
No matter how much I work on making it otherwise,
the hurt, and wonder, and search, and ache remain.
Especially when triggered by four little words.
That little girl, I fear, is with me for life.

Issues?
Yes, I have them.
Don't you?

Little sisters

Two came to stay
I have to be me
I told them I am gay
Later, I heard them whispering
what does that mean, the
little one asked
I don't know, the
other responded
I think that means
she's funny

Funny
what a strange term
but yes, yes, I am.

Time Stands Still

Time stands still
until you walk before a cursed mirror, or
you look at a beloved child.
Then.
Suddenly.
Tempest fugit, is too slow.
Too slow to describe
how quickly time is moving.
Too slow to describe
the rush of emotion like moving ice.
It is difficult to reconcile this disparate
perception of time.
In a flash you wonder;
what happened to the time?
When did it move so silently, so quickly, so
stealthily by?
Where did the time go,
and why does it take life with it?
How did this happen?!
Then you remember a moment.
A frown.
A smile.
A tear.
A person you hold dear.
And, suddenly.
Time stands still.

Seven

Is seven too young?
Too young to know you want to die,
that life is worthless and unfair.

But, old enough.
Old enough to realize that if you die,
that means they win. Old enough to decide
THEY DO NOT DESERVE TO WIN.

Good Times

Remember when Mama took us to the Bahamas?
It was something, flying in that little airplane.
It didn't take us long to realize we were driving
on the wrong side of the road either! I think we lost
some hotdogs and food, swerving to the right side.
We laughed so hard. Mama sure sounds funny when
she cusses.

It was the summer of Sadie, by the Spinners,
the summer of shorts and swimsuits, and conch
fritters. Mama made good conch fritters.
Playing in the pure white sand, amazed at how
the water was blue in the morning and green
in the evening. Remember how clear it was?
You could see all the way to the bottom, but
we found out how deep it was when Stevie
tried to get the money thrown from the ships.
Boy, was it deep. Boy, did we laugh.

Remember we took the boat, headed out to
one of the smaller islands, and didn't know
that Billie built the boat with her own hands?
It started to sink and we had to bail, bail, bail.
I thought we would sink. We didn't. We never do.
But, boy did we laugh.

I will always protect you

It was magnificent.
It was glorious.
The animals were amazing.
I remember Sun City.
The door to our lodging was open.
The monkey made a break for it.
Signs were posted everywhere,
"Don't feed the animals."
Nobody listens. That creates problems.
You yelled and turned to shoo it away.
The monkey turned to you,
chattering and advancing.
You backed up in shock, and fell.
The monkey kept coming.
"Hey", I yelled,
"You get away from my brother,
you son of a bitch!"
I advanced.
The monkey paused and looked at me.
He looked into my eyes
and saw crazy.
The monkey took off in
the opposite direction.
I will always protect you.
All of you.

Star

The warrior woman
entered the room
wading through palpable
despair and doom

The creature child watched warily
as the woman carefully sat on the bed
and gazed into the deep soulless
eyes of the wounded thing
Only she could see
the tiny spark of life that remained
Only she believed
Only she had hope
of saving the beast
before it became a
full-fledged monster

Stella, so aptly named,
you are my star
who brings beautiful light
everywhere you are

Oatmeal

She is being nice
I can look out of the window
I can come out of my room
I can go outside and play
some of these kids are new

Why am I eating so much oatmeal
giant bowls of oatmeal
salad bowls, mixing bowls
lots and lots of oatmeal
oatmeal with butter and sugar
oatmeal with milk and cinnamon
oatmeal with raisins
oatmeal with fruit cocktail
oatmeal
oatmeal
oatmeal

Why am I eating so much oatmeal
Oh, Daddy's coming home
I hate oatmeal

Trey

I call him Trey,
the baby that got away.
We did not meet
until he was in his thirties.

It is very difficult
building bridges,
after the cement
has already hardened.

We try anyway.

Oh Daddy

I
really
thought
you
were going
to do something
with those gymnastics
he said

Oh Daddy
if
I had known
that you noticed
I
would have
won Olympic gold

The Savior

the
one
who
made
it
all
okay
again
until,
it wasn't.
and now,
it will
never
be
okay
again.

DCBR

I am DCBR.
I am damaged.
I am cracked.
I am broken.
I am revived.
This is a tale of triumph,
of overcoming,
of being a victor.
Don't cry for me.
Or, the child that was me,
the child that may have been you.

Damaged
As a child, damaged,
a crack full of fear and angst but,
that's not the crack I speak of.

Cracked
The crack that shows you something beautiful
the first time,
then, has you chasing ghosts and falling off cliffs,
until you realize that, no matter what it promises,
it will never take you there again.
For long.

Broken
Not because life or crack broke me.
But, because one day I looked up from the pit of hell,
after chasing one lie, one ghost too many,
after almost hurting someone over almost nothing.
Really, literally, almost nothing,
because the runner's need was greater than her fear of consequences.
I frightened us both that night.
Later, I cried out,
Lord, I've gone as low as I care to go!

Revived
That's when He saved me.
When I asked.
Not a moment too soon.

Mother and Daughter

An eighteen year old child bride
she cried alone
faced with a mother-in-law who would not look at her
she cried alone
A seventeen year old husband and father off to war
we cried together
moved from the white house to the male boarding house
we cried together
succumbing to the loneliness of the unwanted and alone
we cried together
surrendering to the police who came to take the child
back to the white house
we cried together
reunited after twelve years
we cried together (they always come back to their mother)
unable to express so much love and so much pain
we cried together
unable to repair the damage
we cried together
unable to make it work
we cried together
sick and tired at forty-five
we cried together
gone
far too soon
I cried alone

Varied Responses

If you're going to spend all your money on a woman,
spend it on me.

Does that mean she's funny?

Is there a man in your life?
No.
Is there a woman in your life?
No, but thank you for asking.

We don't care about that, just come home.
Come home to your family.

Love the sinner, hate the sin.
But Auntie, we all fall short of the glory of God.
Do you say that to everyone,
or is it reserved for just the gays?

It has never come up as a topic of discussion.
All is well, as long as it is
the thing that shall never be spoken of.

Chapter Four

Glimpses

One day I looked into a mirror; just some random mirror that I must have passed over a thousand times. But this time I saw someone I never saw before; myself. And it wasn't a carbon copy reflection, no. It was deeper. This time I saw my true self. All of me – the good, the bad, and the ugly. I saw the effects of what the world can do to a person, and what a person can do to himself. One day I looked into a mirror and I saw my soul, battle scars and all. I saw my arms, my hair, my skin; my beautiful chocolate skin.

Some people think we don't dream. They're wrong.

Copyright © 2013
Chocolate Covered Ants
Steven A. Butler, Jr.

Used with permission

Glimpses of a Fractured Soul: Touching Live Wire

It's not the words, words are easy
it's the wondering what to share
it's the worrying about how much
of my soul I should lay bare

How deep into my fractured psyche
will I let you peek
how much of my hard-earned
truth do I let you seek

Every stroke reveals more
opens up a long closed door
every sentence shows you me
they say the telling sets you free

It's not the words, words are easy
it's the wondering what to share
and after laying myself bare
worrying if you'll still be there

So, I show you little glimpses
small doses at a time
of this bruised but healing soul
of this sane, but troubled mind

Are you the one who'll keep my secrets
are you the one to understand
are you the one who'll hold on tightly
never let go of my hand

It's not the words, words are easy
it's the feeling of despair
it's that longing and that hoping
and that praying that you care

It's not the words, words are easy

And yet, discarding fear
and all the other things that mire
I give myself, but careful
it's like touching live wire

Triboluminescence

It had to be this dark to see it,
to write it, to believe it.
The light that comes from breaking,
the light that comes from scratching,
the light that comes from being pulled apart.
Broken, crushed, smashed, ripped, fractured.
Multicolored light, bursts forth, from such a place.
Then, just as promised, beauty for ashes. joy for sorrow.
Walk in the beautiful light.
Triboluminescence.

Because

Because,
even with
all that we lack,
we ourselves,
can be all
that we need.

Adrift

Adrift at sea
no land in sight
the sea waits calmly
waiting for a decision
it offers no guidance
how do you know
the way to salvation

Again

When you open yourself up
and you let people in
the thing that's bound to happen
is that you'll get hurt
again

But this hurt that pains so deeply
this time is not caused by lies
this deep and sorrowful hurt
is caused when someone you love
dies

Oh this journey of humanity
this thing that we call life
with its puzzles and its pitfalls
and its triumphs and its
strife

She would want me to go on
she would want for me to smile
to take one step, then another
til I've gone another
mile

So for her I'll lift my head
and for her I'll soldier on
though she's not with me in body
in my heart she's never
gone

Bad Hair Sunday

I saw the moon yesterday
in the middle of the day
while the sun was shining
like that was the natural way

There she was
big
bold
bodacious
beautiful
Beautiful
for all to see
as though saying:
Who told you
I cannot be here
at this time
Who told you that it is not
my time to shine

I looked for rainbows

Blues and Soul

The sounds of blues and soul
are buried deep within me.
I have embraced the soul,
but always been ashamed
and maybe a little afraid of the blues.

The blues are so telling.
The bass walks around,
stomping, in the front,
leading the way, yet
seeming to support,
and hold the whole thing together.

The guitar wails and moans,
the runs and progression
tell all the secrets of
an aching heart.
Cry baby, cry, it seems to say.
Cry. We will cry together,
and scream,
and plead.
What purer love
can there be, but pain.

The guitar invites the horns,
they dance and parley,
bringing crescendos,
and depths that force you
to close your eyes and see.

The violin takes your hand
and walks with you
to that place.

That's it.
It is all defined by blues
and soul.

But, Realize

The singer
put me on blast talking about
dragging all my
bags from the past

The thing is
I wasn't so
concerned about
the bags

But, what she made me
realize is that carrying
all my bags like that
everyone can see
all my shit

I switched to luggage
I try to leave it home
but, realize,
I have shit

Darkness Came First

I view my life
much like all of creation.
Darkness came first,
and then there was light,
the evening and the morn
were the first day.
Sometimes it has been
darkest before the dawn,
and great sadness has always
preceded great joy.
I have been born into death.
Death of hope.
Death of joy.
Death, of loved ones.
Will I die into life anew?

Few words

I am a woman of few words
and yet
I have so much to say
words swirl
cascade
somersault in my belly
they burn me
they cause me to tremble
wanting their escape
but words betray me
often they do not express what I mean
words are powerful they frighten me
just as they can heal
they can hurt maim and kill
leaving souls and spirits crushed
and bleeding
dying
why does my love sound like anger
why are you angry at me, you ask
I am NOT angry with you
I am afraid
I am afraid that you might be hurt
I'm afraid of losing you

I am angry with myself
for caring enough to BE afraid
I am angry with myself for not being able
not having the words to tell you these things
fear sounds like hate
how can I hate what I do not know
I hate the not knowing
pain is a chameleon
pain hides in plain sight
in words and in silence
that have no way to represent the pain
I am a woman of few words
and yet
I have so much to say
please
look into my eyes
and SEE what I am truly saying
With my few misguided
WORDS
I shall never master words
so please please
look into my heart
And FEEL what I am
TRULY wanting to say

Fallen Leaves, Lost Sisters

Do we hear when each leaf falls,
when each sister is lost?
How can we know? We cannot.
Nor can we count every vein, every triumph
of those we think we know.
We can only do what we can, what we know to do.
We know though,
that every leaf that falls,
every sister that is lost,
leaves behind a legacy, a light,
a space in someone's heart that can be filled by no
other.
Will those we know not of be upset,
feel left out, abandoned or forgotten?
We pray not!
Whether or not we knew of their light,
now extinguished in this realm,
it shines on.
We know.
It shines on.

God's Child

God's Child must be:
a rainbow
a light
a beacon
shining bright

A student
a teacher
a guiding voice
a preacher

The worst
the best
able to lean on Him
and rest

The beginning
the end
the one
who's will He'll bend.

I am God's Child

Handwriting on the Wall

I am afraid to write,
not just the words
but the WAY you write,
reveals so much.
If the line slants up,
you feel happy and light,
but, if it's headed down,
there's depression in sight.
Mix cursive with script, unsure,
unable to make a decision,
the same for mixing upper and lower case.
All small capitals? Uh oh,
Insecure with low self-esteem.
Leaning, looping,
these things reveal so many things
I'm afraid to write.
It may tell someone something
I don't want them to see.

Help

I can't stay here.
They are romancing the stone.
I want.
They make me want.
They make me want more.
No.
I want to get away from the talk.
I must do something different.
Yes.
Yes, my poison was in a different glass.
A rock glass.
That will work.
It works if you work it.
Thank God.
The serenity prayer
helped save my life.
One day at a time.

I Do Me

I do me, better than anyone on earth,
every new morning is like a spring rebirth.

I do me, like the sun in the sky,
nurturing and warming, lifting you high.

Lift your face.
Can't you feel my love radiate?

I do me, like the noonday rain,
I nourish and replenish, and don't try to tame.

I do me, like the waves hugging the shore,
I rush up to meet you, begging for more.
Like that wave, I sweep you away.
Hold on tight, if you want to stay.

I do me, like snow.
Falling gently to cover,
Landing heavily, wet,
Like an exhausted lover.

I do me, like the stars.
Twinkling and smiling,
and inviting you to play.

I do me, like rumbling thunder.
Sometimes soft, sometimes loud,
always rolling through to chase away a cloud.

I do me, like a volcano.
Erupting, hot, sticky, and yes, totally unpredictable,
But I, do me.

So, let me do me,
and you do you,
and **we** will be just fine.
I promise you,
that makes for the very best of times.

I see you, Sister

We are all souls and spirits,
trapped in these decaying bodies.
Some are more trapped than others.

I see you, sister,
staring in despair, into a mirror
that does not reflect back what you see
in your mind's eye, and in your heart.

Most, even I,
cannot begin to imagine how you feel,
the pain of you and those you love,
trying to reconcile what you see,
with what you know.

Others do not see your beauty,
your sensitivity,
your big beautiful heart.

I see you, sister.
You have a beauty most will never know.
You have a courage most will never envision.
You have a strength most will never need.

You are beautiful.
I am proud to call you Sister.

In Retrospect

I watched a timeline slip by,
not even realizing my place in it.

In retrospect,
those were good years.
I should have leapt and ignored the fears.

Oh, my goodness, that was love?
I squandered a gift that was sent from above.

I could have done that? I had the will?
In time I would have acquired the skill?

I should have said, "I love you" more,
not doing so has made me poor.

I should have done that thing right then,
instead of wondering how, or when.

I should have ridden that timeline,
like a surfer boldly through a pipeline.

In retrospect.

Infinity

Time is a construct
within timelessness
Live life like the things
you do go on forever
They do
whether you see them or not
Be careful
especially with words

Praise

I would be remiss,
to not praise my Creator,
so I'd rather do it now,
than to put if off till later.

When He looks at me,
I see love in His eye.
A love that has lifted me,
to soar beyond the sky.

He did not see a crackhead,
someone whose life was done.
He saw me as His daughter,
for whom He sent His Son.

There was no kick when I was down,
there was no angry shout.
He watched and waited patiently
so He could bring me out.

There is no shame I find in Him,
as He has none in me,
so I will share with anyone
just how He set me free.

Praise, and blessed be.

Keep up

I love to rhyme
although some poets
act as though
it is a crime

Noses turned up
mouths in a smirk
as though I don't
understand that
my music
my poetry
does not have to have meter
does not have to stand on its foot
does not have to have pace
it can vacillate
take its time
stop and smell the roses
I may be the only one that gets it

But I understand
and I rhyme anyway
keep up

Lois' Poetry

Silently
I weep
I weep
for raw emotion
poured out
searing
my
very
SOUL

I weep
for love
for love
too strong to hold
for beauty
too
amazing
to
BEHOLD

THIS is the gift
This
is
BEAUTY
FOR
ASHES

My heart is full
I am without speech
Soul behold, beauty for ashes

Reading

Are you reading
what I think I wrote
or
are you reading
what you need to believe

My world colored
by your crayons

Monday Morning

As I sat outside
having my morning respite
a flock of five birds flew overhead
two dragonflies playfully chased each other
one butterfly flitted gliding by
a lone peregrine falcon surfed the air channel high above
a plane roared past in the distance
the palm trees swayed gently in the breeze
I noticed the leaves had finally turned red on
one huge bush due to the cold snap
everything was peaceful
majestic
beautiful
and serene
not a bad Monday morning at all

My Haiku

Since we are here now,
visiting pain. Here, take mine.
I do not want it.

The telling

Gently,
she said,
as she pulled me in
for a hug.
I wrapped my arms
around her.
She felt slight,
almost empty, this vessel,
exquisitely ethereal
more spirit than substance,
spirit before spirit,
light before light.
I looked into her eyes,
to see if she knew
what I now knew.
Soulful eyes gazed back.
She knew, and,
she knew that I knew,
there was no need to ask,
no need for words,
She also knew, that I
knew she has known
for some time,
no doctor need tell her.
No hopeless hope imparted.
This,
her gift to those she loved,
to go swiftly into the night.

My New Rainbow

I've been sad
Mother Nature commiserated
Each day dark and brooding
clouds, no blue sky
no thunder
very little lightning
bucket, upon bucket of tears
On the third day
against the backdrop of
soft white clouds
to the west
a beautiful
brilliant
full
new
rainbow
My neighbor asked
Did you see that rainbow today!
I've never seen one like it
I smiled through my tears
Today,
there are still clouds
but beyond that
the bluest sky
all is well
I will look for
my new rainbow

My Thing

As a poet and artist,
it's my thing,
to step up to the plate,
and take my best swing.

Sometimes I hit the fence,
or I pop up in the air,
I would l never know the score,
if I never took the dare.

Yep, it's my thing.

Night

It seems better at night
when the sun has set and
is no longer sapping energy
the sun seems to rejuvenate
and drain at the same time

The moon calms, offers
a balm to spirit and soul
as well as body
it feels safe and serene
I am less afraid when the
night is inviting me in

That Day

My eyes are leaking.
My soul is weeping.
I know not why.
And yet,
I cry.

It feels of loss.
And yet, of gain.
A deep
and aching,
throbbing pain.

Relationships

I was thinking about circles.
And relationships.
I have a huge outer circle.
But, when did my inner circle
shrink to almost nonexistence?
Was it ever larger than this?

I look at others and their
easy relationships. They send
each other cards, and cookies
without a second thought.
I torture myself over every thought.
When does one get to that carefree place?

I have a feeling getting into my inner circle
is like a sperm looking for that tiny sweet spot
on that one in a million, fortunate egg.
Why is that, I wonder?

Nothing

I have nothing
of consequence
to say today.
It was a day,
and now it is night.

On Being a Poet

I can write a poem sometimes,
quicker than taking a drink.
I can make a new rhyme,
before you can even blink.

You'd think I would be arrogant,
confident, and sure,
but I am rift with feelings
no person should endure.

Is it childish, or too simple,
is it worth the time to read,
I hope it will empower,
planting courage, as a seed.

Will it make the reader laugh,
or rend a heartfelt sigh?
Will it make her leap for joy,
or will it make her cry?

So, when words come to me,
as the first thing in the day,
should I write them down quickly,
or just push the words away?

Words just crop up on their own,
like a random, errant weed,
and to get them down on paper,
seems to be more than a need.

Once the words slow down,
it's like pulling teeth I think,
trying to find them and to shape them
as they drive me to the brink.

Like trying to rhyme with orange,
everybody knows it's true,
doesn't matter how you frame it,
it's impossible to do.

All the rhyming, all the rhythm,
Maybe too much Dr. Seuss,
all the catchy, rhyme books
once devoured as a youth.

I don't want to write the words down,
I don't want others to see,
but the words just soldier round,
taunting, till I set them free.

I will let the words flow out,
I will even write them down,
hoping that when others read them
they won't see me as a clown.

Peaceful

Morning breaks
full of light
the sky
is one large cloud
no blue is sight
it is calm
so still
and quiet
Beautiful
a lone bird
flitters across the sky

I breathe in and out
to an unheard rhythm
Peaceful
THIS is that moment

Just Don't

It is not a good thing
to stay up all night then
expect to greet the world
all chipper and bright
I try to act normal and
calm as a rule but
Invariably I run into a fool

Don't start with me today
about
politics
or religion
or any other
ridiculous thing

Uniquely Mine

My story is
not unique.
But, it is
uniquely, unequivocally,
mine.
I tell it
unapologetically.

Playa

Am I just a player
in other people's lives
When will things start
happening to me, for me
On the fringe
In the periphery
Amongst the shadows
Around the corner
What I need is for things
to come back to the middle
I want to play too

Thy Name

Death,
cancer is thy name.
There was a time when
you had many other
names, and, we have
always known you are
inevitable, but, of late,
the only name
you bear is cancer.
You indiscriminately maim
and claim, young and old
alike.

This is not the equality
we have hoped, prayed,
sweat and fought for,
the kind of equality
that we have bled,
and wept, and died for.

cancer, death is thy name.
We want to change it.
NOW.

Should BE

I should write these things down,
these ideas,
these words,
these fully formed visitations,
these things that magically disappear,
the moment I grab paper and pen.
These things should be remembered.
These things should be told,
should be shouted,
should be said,
should be sung,
Should be.
Should Be.
Should BE.

But, like butterflies,
they flit away,
like butter,
they melt,
No.
Like ice,
like ice they melt.
They melt into water,
then disappear,
without a trace.
Wait.
Let me write this down,
before it disappears.

Sowing

Yes, yes
you reap what you sow
but the thing is
did you know that when you sow
it is much more than
planting a seed

Tend Your Own Garden

Don't go looking 'round girl, someone's always got more; someone's always had it worse, someone's always at the door.

Just tend your own garden, get them weeds, use your hand.
After all that it's done been through, tend it gently as you can.

Others tried to kill your garden, scratch it out by the root, drown it, starve it, burn it, grind it underneath their filthy boot.

Don't be like them, it's your garden, so tend your garden, little girl.

Don't you let it die by your hand, though it seems a hopeless task,
Like a valley too wide, an ocean too deep, a thing too hard to ask.

You have come this far by faith, you've endured the worst storm.
You have hung on tooth and nail, believing for a brighter morn.

Watch it blossom, watch it bloom, watch it break forth and grow.
Hang on through those darkest hours, and you'll have so much to show.

You will quiet all naysayers, like the one that lives inside.
Let your light shine through that bushel, there won't be no need to hide.

Tend your garden, little girl.

Three Things
(Because there are always three things)

You can make it.
You can take it.
You can own this bitch called life.

Say it with me.

I can make it.
I can take it.
I can OWN this bitch called life.

Now go.
Make your mark.

Victor

Growing from strength to strength,
you are making the journey.
Sometimes baby steps,
sometimes giant steps,
sometimes leaps of faith,
sometimes,
faltering backward steps.
You soldier on,
scarred, damaged.
Tender.
You are an enigma to many.
That's okay.
Some will never understand you.
Yet,
you grow,
from victim,
to survivor,
to victor.

OTHER REGAL CREST PUBLICATIONS

Brenda Adcock	Pipeline	978-1-932300-64-2
Brenda Adcock	Redress of Grievances	978-1-932300-86-4
Brenda Adcock	The Chameleon	978-1-61929-102-7
Brenda Adcock	Tunnel Vision	978-1-935053-19-4
Natty Burns	Gospel	978-1-61929-090-7
Sharon G. Clark	Into the Mist	978-1-935053-34-7
Moondancer Drake	Natural Order	978-1-61929-246-8
Moondancer Drake	Ancestral Magic	978-1-61929-264-2
Moondancer Drake	Shadow Magic	978-1-61929-276-5
Jane DiLucchio	Relationships Can Be Murder	978-1-61929-241-3
Jane DiLucchio	Teaching Can Be Murder	978-1-61929-262-8
Jane DiLucchio	Going Coastal	978-1-61929-268-0
Jane DiLucchio	Vacations Can Be Murder	978-1-61929-256-7
Dakota Hudson	White Roses Calling	978-1-61929-234-5
Dakota Hudson	Collateral Damage	978-1-61929-270-3
Kate McLachlan	Hearts, Dead and Alive	978-1-61929-017-4
Kate McLachlan	Murder and the Hurdy Gurdy Girl	978-1-61929-126-3
Kate McLachlan	Rip Van Dyke	978-1-935053-29-3
Kate McLachlan	Rescue At Inspiration Point	978-1-61929-005-1
Kate McLachlan	Return of An Impetuous Pilot	978-1-61929-152-2
Kate McLachlan	Ten Little Lesbians	978-1-61929-236-9
Kate McLachlan	Alias Mrs. Jones	978-1-61929-282-6
Kate McLachlan	Christmas Crush	978-1-61929-196-6
Paula Offutt	To Sleep	978-1-61929-128-7
Paula Offutt	To Dream	978-1-61929-208-6
Patty Schramm	Reflections of Fate	978-1-61929-224-6
Patty Schramm	Souls' Rescue	978-1-935053-30-2
Patty Schramm	Better Together	978-1-61929-154-6
Kelly Sinclair	Getting Back	978-1-61929-242-0
Kelly Sinclair	Accidental Rebels	978-1-61929-260-4
Kelly Sinclair	If the Wind Were A Woman	978-1-61929-272-7
Kelly Sinclair	Roberta's Fire	978-1-61929-300-7
S.Y. Thompson	Under Devil's Snare	978-1-61929-204-8
S.Y. Thompson	Under the Midnight Cloak	978-1-61929-094-5
Barbara Valletto	Pulse Points	978-1-61929-254-3
Barbara Valletto	Everlong	978-1-61929-266-6

Be sure to check out all of our imprints: Blue Beacon Books, Mystic Books, Quest Books, Silver Dragon Books, Troubadour Books, Yellow Rose Books, and Young Adult Books.

About the Author

Mercedes retired from military service after 20+ years. She was one of the first female soldiers selected to attend West Point. Mercedes studied Business and Human Relations at the University of Phoenix. Under the pen name Ms. M, Mercedes is currently published in the erotic anthology *Women In Uniform: Medics and Soldiers and Cops, oh My!* and the poetry anthology Roses Read: Sappho's Corner Poetry Series, Volume 3.

Check out her author page at:
www.regalcrest.biz/author_page.php?author=Lewis_1

She is on Facebook as Mercedes Lewis, Author at:
https://www.facebook.com/GlimpsesOfaFracturedSoul/

Her blog is located at:
https://mercedeslewisblog.wordpress.com

Mercedes is currently Director of Events for the Golden Crown Literary Society, a 501(c)3 non-profit organization for education, adn the recognition and promotion of lesbian literature (http://www.goldencrown.org.)

VISIT US ONLINE AT
www.regalcrest.biz

At the Regal Crest Website You'll Find

- The latest news about forthcoming titles and new releases

- Our complete backlist of titles

- Information about your favorite authors

- Media tearsheets to print and take with you when you shop

- Which books are also available as eBooks.

Regal Crest print titles are available from all progressive booksellers including numerous sources online. Our distributors are Bella Distribution and Ingram.

www.ingramcontent.com/pod-product-compliance
Lightning Source LLC
LaVergne TN
LVHW051645080426
835511LV00016B/2508